LOOKING FORWARD

LOOKING FORWARD

SEEING BEYOND THE OBSTACLES OF LIFE

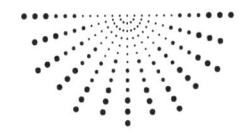

DR. JEFFERY R. WIMBUSH, SR.

IT IS WRITTEN PUBLISHING, LLC

Copyright © 2022 by DR. JEFFERY R. WIMBUSH, SR.

All rights reserved.

All rights reserved. No part of this book may be reproduced in any form or by any electronic or mechanical means, including information storage and retrieval systems, without written permission from the author, except for the use of brief quotations in a book review, magazine, newspaper, website or broadcast.

Scripture quotations, unless otherwise noted, are taken from the King James Version.

Written by: Dr. Jeffery R. Wimbush, Sr.

Cover Design & Photo: Verlisa Wearing

Editor: Belinda DuBose MA Ed.

For copyright permission contact:

Dr. Jeffery R. Wimbush, Sr. at wimbushjeffery@yahoo.com

Library of Congress Cataloging-in-Publication Data

Ebook ISBN: 978-1-956075-10-6

ISBN: 978-1-956075-11-3

Any internet addresses(websites, etc.) and telephone numbers in this book are offered as a resource. They are not intended in any way to be or imply an endorsement of It Is Written Publishing, nor does It Is Written

Publishing vouch for the content of these sites and numbers for the life of this book.

Published in the United States by

It Is Written Publishing, LLC

Atlanta, GA 30213

www.itiswrittenpublishing.net

Manufactured in the United States of America

DEDICATION

Looking Forward: Seeing Beyond The Obstacles of Life is dedicated to God who has seen me through more obstacles than I could ever imagine.

ACKNOWLEDGMENTS

My father, the late Rev. Bennie R. Wimbush, my mother, the late, Leona Wimbush.

To my lovely, wife Christy, and my three children, Chakari, Jeffery Jr. and, Emmanuel and all of my grand- children. Thank God for a loving and supportive family.

To the historical Sweet Home Missionary Baptist Church family, the Heavenly Way Baptist Church, and the Shoal Creek Baptist Church.

Thank God for the major role these three churches have played in my life.

A special thanks to my pastor Dr. James Miller of First Baptist Church of, Warrington Fla. And a special thanks to my mentor Dr. William Flippin, of the Greater Piney Grove Baptist Church of, Atlanta Ga. These two great men helped me and taught me to trust

God and follow the Holy Spirit. I will always be thankful for them.

Last, to all those who helped me to look forward and see beyond the obstacles of life. As I continue to look forward to the future, I am most appreciative.

CONTENTS

INTRODUCTION — xiii

1. THE VISION FACTOR — 1
2. THE FOCUS FACTOR — 19
3. THE FUTURE FACTOR — 37
4. THE AUTHORITY FACTOR — 52
5. THE LEADERSHIP FACTOR — 71

AFTERWORD — 87
THANK YOU — 95
ABOUT THE AUTHOR — 103
ALSO BY DR. JEFFERY R. WIMBUSH, SR. — 107
NOTES — 109

INTRODUCTION

Looking Forward, is about, seeing things in your life one way, and processing them another way. *Looking Forward* is about looking forward to the future and seeing beyond the obstacles that life presents. As leaders, we are to see beyond the obstacles we face. We should always remember that we are not where we will end up. We are seeing things in a positive way or seeing them in a negative way. When a person see things in a negative way it hinders the person's ability to see beyond the obstacles of life. When a person begins to look at things in a positive way, it will help them deal with their present situation in life and to see a better outcome.

INTRODUCTION

Looking Forward is all about seeing the positive in any situation. *Looking Forward* is also about a person pressing their way forward and seeing their desired goal accomplished.

The Vision factor is something that every leader deals with. A good leader understands that the vision is yet for an appointed time. Therefore, the vision needs to be written and made plain. He or she also knows that they will perish without a vision. The visionary leader knows what his or her focus is. Because obstacles will arise, the focus factor is also important. Staying focused, keeps a person tuned in to the present and looking toward the future. The future factor is what keeps the visionary leader motivated. He or she has a glimpse of what the future can be or will be.

1
THE VISION FACTOR

A vision is the compelling force that drives an individual, an organization or the church. Without a vision, the individual or organization, and even the church will surely fail. *"Where there is no vision, the people perish: but he that keep the law is happy"* (Proverbs 29:18). Any leader without a vision cannot lead their followers no farther than they can visualize. A visionary leader understands not only the importance of the vision, but where the vision comes from, how it motivates, and how it is to be communicated. "If it is true that great vision inspires great people and organizations, the crucial task for leaders is to develop the loftiest vision possible for their organizations. Walt Disney had a broad vision-to make people happy-and he redefined the entertainment business. Henry Ford sought to democratize the automobile, and the result was a prodigiously successful automotive empire. George Marshall's vision was to develop the mightiest army in the world; he began with an army of 200,000 men in 1939 and by 1945 he had created a force of 8.3 million. Bill Gates had a vision that every computer in the world would use Microsoft software; his success is legendary. When people consider the examples of great business leaders, they feel pressured to develop grandiose that will likewise propel their organization to greatness. But where do leaders find visions that inspire people and unite them to great accomplishments? There are many sources from which leaders draw their vision." These sources are called help.

LEADERS SOMETIMES DRAW THEIR VISION from other leaders such as pastors, teachers, CEO's coaches, consultants, counselors, mentors, etc..... The visionary leader learns from God and other visionary leaders. These other visionary leaders are men or women who have achieved a certain level of success. Therefore, the visionary leader becomes a visionary follower and accomplishes their God given vision. Any visionary follower will eventually become a good visionary leader. In order to be a good visionary leader, you need to be a good visionary follower. Therefore, visionary leaders follows the greatest visionary leader of all. That is the Lord Jesus Christ!

VISION WILL COME ALIVE WHEN THE visionary leader knows that the vision comes from God and that it is divine. "Yet many Christian leaders adopt the world's approach to vision and miss out on God's way. In seeking to serve God, they inadvertently try to take on the responsibility of God. The truth is, God is on a mission to redeem humanity. He is the only one that knows how to do it. Leaders must understand as Christ has done, that their role is to seek the Father's will and to adjust their lives to him. Too often Christian leaders operate under a false sense of assurances they are seeking God's will. Being proactive by nature, leaders want to rush into action. As a result, they do not spend enough time to hear clearly from God. Instead, they simply have a cursory moment of prayer and then make their plans. They seek out a few relevant Scriptures and hurry into the goal setting phase, "falsely confident that because incorporated prayer and scriptures into their goal setting process, their plans are of God." Wise visionary leaders have seen too many obstacles to look forward without the guidance of the Holy Spirit. He or she also defines leadership.

THE DEFINITION OF VISIONARY LEADERSHIP must lead every visionary leader. There are many definitions of leadership. The ability to move a person or a group of people from where they are to where they need to be is one definition. Another definition is the ability to influence one or more persons to accomplish a certain goal. Dr. John Maxwell said, *"Leadership is all about influence and that is it."*

LOOKING FORWARD

There are many other scholars that have defined leadership, but the definition I define leadership to be is, "Leadership is the God given ability to influence a person or a group of persons to accomplish a God given mission." Since the vision is God given, the visionary leader must understand how important the vision is to God. He or she must also trust God no matter what the outcome looks like. The visionary leader does not look to just conquer the obstacles they visualize, but they must also look forward to conquering the obstacles they do not visualize. They understand the importance of their vision to their ministry and calling. A clear and compelling vision provides energy to the people and the organization or church. This type of leadership ignites the fire that drives the vision forward. The visionary leader's vision creates a cause in the followers' lives. This gives the followers a divine sense of purpose. When followers have a divine sense of purpose, they are not afraid to take risks. The risk may be big, but the visionary leader sees a bigger God. Risk taken by the leader, also legitimize the leader's position. They can see beyond the obstacle of life and see a clear and compelling future. Their vision is a snap shot of what the future will look like. A compelling vision also energizes the leadership and the organization. As difficult as ministry can be, the energy that come from the vision sustains the ministry. When the vision is sustained and communicated well, it can become a clear compelling picture of the future and what it can be and must be. Developing a compelling vision has two processes. The first process is the preparation stage. This starts with the leader envisioning prayer over the desired goal. Everything the visionary leader does, should start with prayer and end with prayer. This allows God to take the lead in the preparation process. The next step is the process step. In the process step the vision is expanded to your mission statement, and it identifies the core value. The visionary leader must communicate the vision and their action must demonstrate their faith in the vision. "The sermon is the primary means for casting the vision. Whereas, the mission communicates well on paper or written on a business card, the vision is best expressed through spoken communication. The power of the vision is in hearing it preached, not reading it. You can

LOOKING FORWARD

discern this by reading Martin Luther King Jr.'s great vision message and then listen to it. He communicates with great passion and conviction. This is the key! Today's preachers who believe in their visions should demonstrate passion and conviction. If the pastor struggles as a vision caster, the church may be in trouble. That is the bad news. The good news is that he can learn to grow in his vision-casting ability. To do this, he must first discover his passion ---he will communicate best what he is passionate about! It is his passion that motivates him. And he must be sure he is embracing the right passion. My research and experience as a church consultant have shown that passion for the Great Commission must be at the core of the pastor's vision. The thought of people accepting and then growing in Christ should deeply move the leader. If it does, he will not have difficulty communicating his vision." The vision should be communicated with such passion, that it creates urgency and establish a vision community. These are the followers that trust God and leadership to accomplish a God given vision. Now that the process is in motion, it is time communicate the vision.

DR. JEFFERY R. WIMBUSH, SR.

. . .

"THE GROUNDWORK IS COMPLETED. THE pastor and other key leaders have spent time in personal preparation, there is a growing and widely shared sense of urgency it is not acceptable to maintain the status quo, and a small and diverse group of members has formed to lead the change process. But in what direction will they lead? The difference between recognizing a need for change ("What we are doing is not working") and agreeing on the shape and direction of the change is enormous.

THE CHANGE PROCESS ULTIMATELY REVOLVES around the clear discernment and articulation of God's vision for the congregation. As we discuss below, vision is preceded by an understanding of mission and it is followed by a detailed description of the vision path. In many ways, achieving clarity and consensus around God's vision is the most important part of the change process. Vision should establish an identity for the congregation – what we are, what we are not, and what we expect to become in three to five years. The earlier stages prepares the congregation's leaders for understanding God's vision. The subsequent stages are all a result of following the vision." To communicate the vision, the leader needs to develop an explicit communication strategy. This will explain how communication is to be carried out. Terms and phrases that have special meaning should communicate to the congregation. Once this is established the terms should be repeated repeatedly. The visionary leader should always look for creative ways to communicate their vision. Dr. John Maxwell teaches on the communication shift a lesson on directing to connecting. He teaches that directing is authoritative and connecting is collaborative. Directing is talking where connecting is listening. When you direct people you enlist them and when you connect to people you empower them. In order to connect with people, you need to find common ground. One way to find common ground is humility. Humility is one way of letting people know that you need them. Effort is another way to connect to people. This is when you go out your way to connect with other people. Being someone that people can trust also will help find common ground. Listening is one of the best ways to find common ground and encouragement gives people oxygen for their soul.

T̲ʜ̲ᴇ̲ ̲ᴋ̲ᴇ̲ʏ̲ ̲ᴛ̲ᴏ̲ ̲ꜰ̲ᴜ̲ʟ̲ꜰ̲ɪ̲ʟ̲ʟ̲ɪ̲ɴ̲ɢ̲ ̲ʏ̲ᴏ̲ᴜ̲ʀ̲ ̲ʟ̲ɪ̲ꜰ̲ᴇ̲'ꜱ̲ ̲ᴘ̲ᴜ̲ʀ̲ᴘ̲ᴏ̲ꜱ̲ᴇ̲ is to live out your vision. Jesus said *"For this reason was I born, and for this came I into the world, to testify to the truth"* (John 18:37). All of us were born to do something special in life, because everyone is born with a unique vision. As your vision becomes your purpose, it will fire up your passion. When your passion is ignited, it stirs up your gift which will make away for you. *"A man's gift makes room for him and brings him before great men"* (Proverbs 18:16). A visionary leader develops his or her gifts. They understand that they must develop their gift and stir it up. *"Therefore, I remind you to stir up the gift of God which is in you through the laying on of my hands"* (2 Timothy 1:6). That is why it is not only important to understand how important a vision is, but also the power it brings to the leader and the leadership team.

. . .

LOOKING FORWARD

SINCE VISION CREATES PURPOSE AND VISION and purpose comes from God, then God created you with a purpose and a vision. It is up to each individual, to stir that gift up and realize all the good things God has in store for them. Since everything comes from God, it is God who will see that the vision comes to past. *"I am God, and there is no other; I make known the end from the beginning, from ancient times, what is still to come. I say: My purpose will stand, and I will do all that I please"* (Isaiah 46:9-10). As you continue to follow the Holy Spirit, your vision becomes a reality. You See the vision as if it were already happening. Too Often we say, greater is He that is in me, than He that is in the world, and only to look for visions from the world. You will not only find God's vision in you, but you will also find His will for your life. God is able, to do abundantly above all that we could ever ask or think, according to the power that works in us. We are to use that power or gift to complete our mission and to bring glory to the kingdom of God. *"That everyone may eat and drink and find satisfaction in all his toils-this is the gift of God"* (Ecclesiastes 3:13). This is when we do the work that God created us to do. When we do what God has called us to do, we will find fulfillment in life and in ministry. To withstand your purpose and vision, you must sustain the will of God for your life. I like this definition: "Vision is foresight with insight based on hindsight." We have insight into God's purpose for us based on what we know God has accomplished in eternity. Vision is a glimpse of our future that God has purposed. We do not know all the details of how our purposes will unfold, but we see their "ends" because God reveals them to us in the vision, he gives us. That is why we can be confident that the vision will come to pass.

SUPPOSE YOU DO NOT HAVE THE MONEY YOU need to fulfill your vision. God says to you *"I've already been where you are going, and you will have everything you need."* He tells us that our visions will be completed, and this gives us courage and keeps us from being depressed when things don't look as if they will work out. We know as believers that *"all things will work together for the good to those who love God and to those who are called to his purpose." "We are God's workmanship, created in Christ Jesus to do good works, which God prepared in advance for us to do"* (Ephesians 2:10). Doing good work does not lead to salvation. Jesus Christ is the only way to gain salvation. He gives us salvation to carry on the work of discipleship and to fulfill our mission here on earth. He declared that his disciples shall do greater works because he was going to the father. A visionary leader understands that the vision is to be shared. That is why communication is so important. When sharing your vision always remember that some get it and some do not, some will, and some will not. This can be disappointing but remember that the vision is given to you to cast, but the followers need to catch the vision. Waiting on the followers to catch the vision, can be frustrating if you are impatient. Therefore, it is imperative that the visionary leader have a strong relationship with God. This is important, because any vision from God is too big to do alone and you need people to help you fulfill the vision. Most of all you need God to complete the vision and the aid of the Holy Spirit.

DR. JEFFERY R. WIMBUSH, SR.

. . .

THE VISIONARY LEADER WILL FACE MANY obstacles trying to accomplishing the desired goal. The Holy Spirit gives the visionary leader the wisdom to avoid obstacles or the wisdom to handle the obstacles he or she faces. These obstacles no matter what they may be, are only obstructions that keep us from reaching our goal. That is why it is important to pinpoint your goal. No matter what obstruction take place, the visionary leader must be specific about what they want to accomplish. This will help to identify the objective of success and clear up the difference between the mission, value, and vision. The vision is a snapshot of what the church or the organization can look like. It is a glance of what the future can be. The vision is also what creates energy and gives cause to those in the organization. It also sustains the ministry and legitimizes leadership. A visionary leader will foster risk taking and motivate giving. *"The information that is available indicates that pastors and congregations are struggling with the vision concept. For exam-*

ple, in commenting on pastors and their vision", George Barna writes, But when we ask these pastors, *"Can you articulate God's ministry for your church?"* we found that roughly ninety percent of them could articulate a basic definition of ministry. But only two percent could articulate the vision for the church. David Goetz writes, *"In leadership studies, however, pastors indicated that conflicting vision for the church was their greatest source of tension and the top reason they were terminated or forced to resign."* Clearly vision differs from mission and imperative to the visionary leader.

THE MISSION IS WHAT THE ORGANIZATION OR the church is suppose to be doing. The vision gives purpose because it is broader and can change. The mission does not change. It answers the, what question while the vision answers the why question. The mission can conscience verse unconscious or it can be personal verse organizational. It can also be a shared mission or an unshared mission because there are many forms of missions.

Other forms like, correct verse incorrect and actual verse aspirational must be considered when developing a mission. No matter what form is used it must tie into the Great commission found in Matthew 28. Let me use the Christian church as an example. The assignment that the young Jewish rabbi, Jesus, gave His followers two thousand years ago – *"go into all the world and preach the good news"* (Mark 16:15)-is called the Great Commission. It is the co-mission, the joint or corporate mission of the church. It is every Christian's mission. What sincere church does not want to preach the Gospel to every person, bring people to God, and equip people to minister to others? Therefore, if a church thinks that their vision is to preach the Gospel, then it has a mistaken idea of vision. It knows its mission, but it has not yet found its true vision, at one thing that distinguishes it from all other churches. When the church or the organization, identify its mission, then it must identify its mission statement. When the organization or church decides on the mission statement, they must remember that it should be no longer than three part and T-shirt ready.

. . .

THE VALUES ARE IMPORTANT TO THE organization and they differ from the vision. The values tell the organization or the church what is important and why they do what they do. Values also determine the ministry distinctive and dictate personal involvement. The values will communicate a clear picture of what is important. When values are communicated properly the people will be inspired to action. They also influence the behavior of the organization and they embrace good change. When the visionary leader understands these three and their differences, he can stay focused on completing the assignment. Visionary leaders succeed because they know what they want to succeed in. They are directed by a clear and compelling vision that keeps them from being distracted. Visionary leaders see the future they expect. They have a clear picture of something that can be but is not yet reality. He or she knows that it is God working in their life to complete the vision. *"Now unto Him that is able to do above and abundantly all that we ask or think according to the power that works in us"* (Ephesians 3:20). As the visionary leader moves forward in faith, God's power is activated in their lives and their vision. This is when the visionary leader understands their purpose and their walk with God. They see beyond the obstacles of life, looking forward to the future.

2
THE FOCUS FACTOR

The visionary leader needs to stay focused on the vision he or she has been given. Many things could happen when leaders follow the vision from God. *"We wrestle not against flesh and blood, but against principalities, against powers, against the rulers of darkness of this world, against spiritual wickedness in high places"* (Ephesians 6:12). The enemy will do everything that can be done to kill, steal or destroy your vision. He will send every obstruction he can to stop you. The visionary leader needs to stay focused and know the tricks and voices of the devil. As visionary leaders, we must take ownership of the vision that God has given us and let him that stole; steal no more. Dr. Flippin stated, *"You will never accomplish your vision in life, until you claim your vision as your own."* We know we take better care of things that belong to us. I am convinced the reason many never see their dreams come to pass is because they believe the vision belongs to someone else. Such as starting a business is someone else's job or chartering a school should be accomplished by someone else. The person of your dream is supposed to have a family with someone else. The new home you are supposed to purchase cannot be bought in this economy and market. I challenge you not to focus on the external environment. Rather remain focused on the destiny only you can perceive. The vision may not make sense to someone else; or to you but it "belongs to you." You must take ownership of your vision and stay focused on it. There are five focus factors I learned from Dr. Samuel Chand. They are personal focus, which helps to discover how God is guiding you as a visionary leader. You also learn how to handle internal shifts and maintain focus. The platform focus is where you construct an effective vision. Habakkuk 2:2 says, *"Write*

LOOKING FORWARD

the vision and make it plain on tablets, that he may run who reads it." This is a part of the planning process. You must develop a concrete plan for your vision. If you fail to plan for your vision, then you plan for your vision to fail. God gives the vision to the visionary leader and the visionary leader made the plans. Then God direct the visionary leader to accomplish the desired outcome. The visionary leader knows what the future will be like. Ideas are seeds of destiny planted by God in the minds of humankind. When ideas are cultivated, they become imagination. Imagination, if it is watered and developed, becomes a plan. Finally, if a plan is followed, it becomes a reality. However, when a person receives an idea from God, it must be cultivated, or the idea often goes away. If that person does Never work on the idea, God will give it to someone else. Inevitably, if the second person takes the idea, creates a plan, and works on it, the first person will become jealous because he or she had the idea first! Yet it is not just having an idea that is important, the ideas needs to have a plan if there's going to be a reality. The vision blueprint tells you where you are headed and who you are to become. Without your plan, God has nowhere to start from or lead you. He has only you, until you give him your plan.

THE VISIONARY LEADER HAS A PASSION FOR their vision engraved in their heart. When this happens, the visionary leader has discovered something worth more than life itself. The Lord Jesus Christ said *"If any man will come after me, let him deny himself, and take up his cross, and follow me. For whosoever will save his life shall lose it: and whosoever will lose his life for my sake shall find it. For what is a man profit, if he shall gain the whole world, and lose his own soul? Or what shall a man give in exchange for his soul? For the Son of man shall come in the glory of his Father with his angels; and then he shall reward every man according to his works. Verily I say unto you, there are some standing here, which shall not taste of death, till they see the Son of man coming in his kingdom"* (Matthew 16:23-28). Jesus saw something worth putting his whole heart into. He never let his eyesight limit what his heart saw. He followed the vision God gave him all the way to the cross. He saw something worth dying for. Jesus said, *"I came forth from the Father, and I am come into the world, again, I leave the world to go to the Father"* (John 16:28). His vision plan identified who he was and where he was headed. He knew completing the task would be hard, but his mind was made up to do his Father's will. Jesus used the platform that God had given him to do great things. What are you doing with the platform that God has given you? All you need to do is have a starting point and a plan for your vision. If you stay focused, the vision that God gave you will bloom right before your eyes. "You do not need to be big to think great thoughts. You need to think great thoughts to become big".

THE THIRD THING THAT DR. CHAND discussed was the people focused. The visionary leader knows that he or she does not end up with the people they started with. Developing other leaders is the best way to help get to the desired goal. "If churches are going to last, it's imperative that they develop people into the leaders they need. Raising up leaders is a more effective way to minister and efficiently using resources. But development only occurs when leaders realize that other people can bring the ministry to a place they could never reach alone". Some leaders never develop others because of the fear of vulnerability or pressing demands. There is the threat of a repeated pattern and past disappointments. Scripture illustrates how disappointments might keep us from developing other leaders. When Moses was on Mt. Sinai receiving the Ten Commandments, Aaron was down below overseeing Israel's wild fraternity party. When Moses returned, he found that the leader he trusted had seriously blown it. When Pastors raise up leaders, there will always be a leader who may disappoint them. Too often, it is the leaders that Pastors spend the most time with who can cause them the greatest hurt. And because a pastor may have been hurt, they may not continue developing leaders. "If we are not willing to encounter an Aaron who might disappoint us, we will never find the Joshua who will carry on after us". As leaders, we must remember that someone saw more in us than we saw in ourselves. Someone believed in us when we did not believe in ourselves. No matter how often we are disappointed, we must see what God see in others, looking for the next follow first leader. The follow first leader has learned to follow and is ready to lead, yet they have a follower's mind set. *"And when he had called the people unto him with his disciples also, he said unto them, whosoever will come after me, let him deny himself, and take up his cross and follow me"* (Mark 8:34). Jesus knew that the disciples would run off and desert Him, He knew that they would doubt Him, He knew that they would deny Him, and that one of them was a devil and would betray him. Despite knowing this, Jesus went on being about his Fathers business of making disciples for the kingdom of God. When you are people focus, you will continue to follow the great commission, no matter how difficult it may be to develop or disciple others. It is hard to help others grow into the person they can become, when it's hard for them to believe in themselves.

DEALING WITH PEOPLE AND THEIR WAY OF thinking, can be difficult. Their culture is another factor, because as the culture changes, the individual changes. "Maybe you are going through a hard time right now and you are disheartened. You have lost your vision edge and unable to see beyond the obstacles of life. Perhaps this is because of your surroundings. Sometimes, the environment is not the best for fostering vision. What people say to us is not always encouraging and can be very discouraging. I have been tempted to be disillusioned and discouraged often. Even though we know that the discouraging things we see and hear are temporary, they still can distress and depress us. We must keep our vision constantly before us, however, because the visions in our heart, it greater than our environments. "God gave us vision so we would not live by what we see." That is why we walk by faith and not sight.

As we continue to look forward beyond the obstacles we see, be procedural focused. This is the system or program that guides the organization or the church regularly. It is important to focus on this because the procedures must match the DNA of the organization or church. "Whatever systems we adopt should always be contextualized to our community. It is not enough to know that it played well in Peoria; there needs to be a match to our own organization. By focusing on why a church or organization does something instead of focusing on what they are doing, we can facilitate this matching and customization. This simple change in our thinking by helping us to grasp the essence of a procedure or program, which enables us to have the new ideas we will need to build an effect system. This system must not limit our vision, because the vision is bigger than the system or procedure. The vision is bigger because it comes from God and God is bigger than any system or procedure. The last step to this process is to be problem focused. I tell my spiritual sons that have gone out to pastor to be problem focused. When they are on their way to minister the word of God, be ready to deal with three major things. If they deal with one thing that Sunday, then they have had a good day. There may be a personal crisis, public crisis, pressure crisis or a problem. All of these can lead to a serious problem. I talked about conflict in the book leading forward overcoming the obstacles of life, in the chapter on fellowship. All leaders deal with problems.

THE VISIONARY LEADER MUST STAY FOCUSED because he or she knows that their vision is the key to fulfilling life's purpose. Staying focused, gives the visionary leader a reason to live and the vision tells them where they are headed. "When I speak to groups of people about vision, whether it is in the context of business, government, or the church, I always emphasize the following truth because I believe that it is crucial for each one of them to understand: The poorest person in the world is a person without a dream. Visionary leaders that can't see beyond their obstacles are not normal and will never be satisfied living a normal life. Their life will be full of frustration until they fulfill their dream. Visionary leaders also have a unique vision because the vision comes from a unique God. So many times, people have come to me and ask the question, what is my ministry or what does God want me to do? I tell them that they need to ask God that question. I can give them an assignment in the church, but I can't give them a vision. I can share my vision with them and pray that they will catch it. All of us was put here with a purpose and to do something that is only for us to do. As we go through life, we should want to end up saying what Jesus said on the cross *"It is finished"* (John 19:30). Too many times people never become the person that God wants them to be or accomplish the things God has planned for them. *"For I know the thoughts I think toward you, said the Lord, thoughts of peace, and not of evil, to give you an expected end"* (Jeramiah 29:11). When you realize that God has a purpose for your life and what that purpose is, then becomes your passion.

MOST PEOPLE NEVER DISCOVER THEIR purpose or their passion in life. Your vision will give you drive and passion for God. Because of this, no matter how big or hard the vision is, a visionary leader will follow their vision until it is finished. They understand that the vision is theirs, but it came from God. "For we know that all things work together for good, to those that love the Lord. To those that are called according to His purpose. You will have those that never see your vision or their own vision. Then there are those that ask what in the world is going on or what just happened. Then there is the visionary leader that stayed focused and make things happen. They are not all over the place or in everyone else's lane. They stayed focused on their own gift and what God has called them to do. The visionary leader doesn't try to operate out of another person's gift.

He or she realizes that operating out of someone else gift will not work for them. *"A man's gift will make room for him"* (Prov. 18:16). It is not in his wits, or education, but what God has placed on the inside or revealed through the Holy Spirit. "Education in itself, doesn't guarantee anything; it is your gift that is the key to your success. The second part of Proverbs 18:16 says, *"A man's gift... brings him before great men"* (NKJV). You don't realize that the gift that you are sitting on is loaded. The world will not move over because you are smart. Whenever you exercise your gift, however, the world will not only make room for you, but it will also pay you for it. Anyone-yourself included- who discovers his or her gift and develops it will become a commodity. If you are a young person in high school or college that's planning your career, don't carry out what people say will make you wealthy. Do what you were born to do because that is where you will make your money. No matter how big the world is, there is a place for you in it when you discover and manifest your gift. I have told people over and over, whatever gift they may have, that is what they should work out of. Don't try to be anyone else or operate out of anyone else's gift. You need to discover your own gift and use it to make room for you. The gift is there, you just need to discover it and learn how to use it.

WHAT YOU WILL FIND OUT WHEN YOU discover your gift is that it was there all along. While you were focusing on all these other things and other people's gifts, yours was just lying there. While everyone else was happy and prospering, you were wondering why you were stuck in the same cycle. That is because you were not operating in your God given gift. *"A gift is as a precious stone in the eyes of him that hath it: whithersoever it turns, it prospers"* (Prov. 17:8). When a person realize that God has given them a vision and a purpose in life, they can understand the power of that vision and get stirred up to accomplish great things. *"Wherefore I put thee in remembrance that you stir up the gift of God, which is in thee by the putting on of my hands. For God has not given us the spirit of fear; but of power, and of love, and of sound mind"* (2Timothy 1:6-7). That is when your life will become meaningful and you will see the power of your vision. You will then understand why the vision is so important to your success. It will also help you to discover your life purpose and help you to live it out. Your vision will help you to see beyond the obstacles you face and stay on course. That is when you will live the life you were meant to live.

SINCE IT IS GOD THAT GIVES THE DREAM OR vision, then God love to see the visionary in action. Joseph the son of Jacob was known as the dreamer. Joseph was Jacob's favorite son and he made him a coat of many colors. Joseph dreamed a dream and told his brothers. His brothers hated him even more because of the dream and the coat that his dad had made for him. Joseph teaches us you cannot share your dreams with everyone. This also include some family members. When Joseph told his dad the second dream, even his dad got offended. One day when Joseph went to look for his brothers in Dothan. When he found them in Dothan, they saw him coming, they conspired to kill him. People will get jealous enough to hurt you or kill you over your vision. When Joseph arrived to where his brothers were, they stripped him of his coat that his dad had made. They planned to kill Joseph, but Ruben spoke up. They put Joseph in a pit that had no water. When a band of Ishmeelites came, Judah decided that it would be best to sell Joseph to them, and his brothers went along with him. Joseph was sold for twenty pieces of silver and carried down to Egypt. People will sell you out because of your dream. When Ruben returned and found that Joseph was not in the pit. He and his brothers took Joseph coat and killed a kid goat and dip the coat in the goat blood. They carried the coat back to their dad and told him that a wild beast had killed Joseph. While Joseph was in Egypt, he eventually became governor of the land when the famine hit the land. The dreamer who was laughed at, plotted on and sold into slavery, is now the one God used to save the family. Eventually, the vision that Joseph had finally came to pass. *"For the vision is yet for an appointed time, but at the end it shall speak, and not lie though it tarry, wait for it; but it will surely come, it will not tarry"* (Habakkuk 2:3).

GOD ALLOW JOSEPH TO GO THROUGH ALL these obstacles, yet he protected him because of the vision he had given him. Joseph never lost hope or his faith. Joseph knew that his vision would come to pass. God loves the visionary, and He protects the vision and the visionary. God loves the dreamer that dreams big and can see beyond the obstacles they see. Through it all Joseph stayed focused on the vision he had seen as a young man. Because of this dreamer, Jacob and his family. The visionary leader stay should focus on the vision.

LOOKING FORWARD

The visionary leader might have the vision, but the vision is for more than just the dreamer. It will affect all those that are involved and catch the vision. If you have a true vision, it will build people up rather than tear people down. Many people fail because the loose focus when things do not go the way they planned. You need to be mindful that the vision came from God and he has the plan of how the vision will come to pass. No matter how many obstacles you face, stay focused on what God has shown you and what God has said to you. Always remember that no great work was done by one individual. Work with people going in the same direction you are. Those want to spend your time wisely. Birds of a feather will flock together, and you will become like those who you spend your time carelessly with. This is called the Law of Association. The visionary leader should spend the majority of their time, with people that is a positive influence and spend their minor time with people that is negative. Negative people will do three things that cause the visionary leader to lose their focus. Because the vision is bigger than you and them, their negativity will discourage you. Because it is a

God given vision the enemy will throw so many obstacles at you that the negativity will depress you. The third thing that the enemy will do is to try his best to distract you from reaching your goal. The positive people will bring three things to the table when they catch the vision. They will be enthused about where the church or the organization is headed. Positive people will bring a burst of energy that will keep the vision alive. Positive people will also bring the effort to work along with the visionary leader to see that the vision is complete. So, a visionary leader needs to stay focused on their desired goal, looking beyond all the obstacles they face.

3
THE FUTURE FACTOR

The future factor is simply seeing yourself, situations, circumstances, and even life beyond the place you are at. It is a glimpse of what the next day, month or year will look like. When the leadership team look at what the future will look like, they, as leaders, must be ready for the change. The change readiness starts with the leader's mindset. Dr. Chand stated *"What will the future look like?"* It is a question we in a position of authority need to think through carefully. We need to help those who serve under us and with us to understand that we can't function effectively with the methods and mind-set of the past. As I wrote that last statement, it made me wonder. How many people refused to buy TV dinners and cake mixes forty years ago. As late as 1999, several of my friends said, "You will never catch me in public walking around with one of those cell phones". Obviously, people do change their minds, and that alters their behavior. Today I can see some of those once resistance friends talking on their cell phones as they walk across the church parking lot or through the mall. My point is that we count on most people to make abrupt paradigm changes. We need to remind ourselves that we're not trying to adjust and alter just so, see we are different. Our changes need to have a purpose for us to revise our thinking. The major purpose for us as future faith people is to become a more effective witness for Jesus Christ".

AS A WITNESS FOR JESUS, WE MUST BE prepared for change. Future first leaders should always look ahead to the return of Jesus Christ. Even though we are in the world, we are not of this world. We look to the future when Jesus Christ will reign in the

LOOKING FORWARD

kingdom of God here on earth. We are not to be entangled in the affairs. We know like Abraham, that God has so much more in store for his people. *"By faith Abraham, when he was called to go out into a place, which he should afterward receive for an inheritance, obeyed: and he went out not knowing where he went. By faith he sojourned in the land of promise, as in a strange country, dwellings in tabernacles with Isaac and Jacob, the heirs with him of the same promise. For he looked for a city which hath foundations, who builder and maker is God"* (Hebrews 11:8-10). As we travel the land looking to develop other future leaders, we have to ask ourselves "What did I do today to ready myself for the future? Will yesterday's preparations carry me through tomorrow? Is there some new preparation I need to make today that will carry me through tomorrow." A future thinker or visionary, will always try to be prepared for what is next. There will always be a next, we just don't always know what the next will be. We can trust God to lead us to and through the next step of life. Wisdom tells us to *"trust in the Lord with all our heart, and lean not to our own understanding, but in all our ways ac-*

knowledge Him, and He shall direct our path" (Proverbs 3:5-6). We must trust God just as Abraham did. We do not just trust for our present condition; we also trust God for our future. Abraham was willing to give up his son Isaac when God told him to offer him for a sacrifice (Genesis 22:1-19). However, God did not allow Abraham to take his son's life, but had a ram in the bush. God always has a ram in the bush or make a way of escape. Abraham sacrificed the ram to God. God not only provides, but he also spares us as he did Isaac. Think of all the stuff you went through or dealt with from the age of reasoning until now. You will have to agree that God not only provided, but he also spared us.

God did not take Isaac's life because He gave Abraham the command to test his faith. Life will be filled with tests. Every time you fail the test you either retake the test or give us as a failure. I talked about the failure factor in the book Leading Forward, Overcoming the Obstacles of Life. For the future leader, failure is not an option. We know that the just shall live by faith, and that we walk by faith.

LOOKING FORWARD

Future thinkers live a life filled with faith. Abraham life was filled with faith. In Genesis12, at God's command, Abraham left home not knowing where he was going. In the spring of two thousand God spoke and told me to resign from being pastor of the Heavenly Way Baptist Church. I struggled with it because the church had grown tremendously and been remolded and debt free in five years. I thought that was where I was to stay. They contacted me to preach and called me to pastor. It seemed everything is going fine. I worked fifteen minutes from my house as a warehouse manager. The church was fifteen to twenty minutes from my house, and God said to resign. The second week God told me to resign. I said Okay, but I did not type up the resignation letter. That Sunday I was uneasy all day. After service, Deacon Brownlee asked if I was okay and I told him yes and he replied, "you are wrestling with God about something." Deacon Canady called me that night and said that he believe God is moving his pastor. I shared a little with him and we prayed. That Wednesday night. Pastor John Adams showed up at our bible study. It was an honor to see this senior pastor at our bible study. After bible study He asked could he talk. You know I'm feeling Good now, we had a good bible study and now Pastor Adams wants to meet with me. We went in my study and sat down. We asked about one another's family. Then he said Rev. I enjoyed bible study. I said, "I'm glad you did." Then he said, "now Wimbush, you know I don't do this often." I was like what is it now. He said, "God has told you twice that it is time to resign and you going up the road." I said, yes sir, I know I have to resign, but I just don't know where I'm going. He said, "you are going up the road." We talked a little longer and he left. As he walked off, I knew I had to resign. I typed up my resignation letter that weekend and read over it. As I was putting it in the envelope, God said, "type one up for your job as well." I was stunned. I told my wife what God said. She asked, "what was I going to do." I responded that I had better do what God said. I resigned from the church that Sunday and my job that Monday. All of my friends thought I had lost my mind. I was at home praying all day Tuesday. We had just bought two brand new cars; a house note and three children. I simply believed what God

LOOKING FORWARD

said and it was confirmed by Pastor Adams. Just as Abraham believed the covenant God made with him in Genesis Ch. 12, 13, and 15. The next morning Deacon Wendell Gay called me and introduced himself as the chairman of the Sweet Home Missionary Baptist Church. One of the deacons (Deacon Johnny Sims) had heard me do a eulogy and recommended me. They did not know that I had resigned from Heavenly Way. He asked, "When do, I think I could come." I asked him, "When do you want me to come." He said, "I wish you could come this Sunday the guy we had coming backed out." I said, "that I could make some arrangements". Pastor Tyler filled in for me and did a great job. I went on to Sweet Home and preached. Pastor Adams was right; I have been driving up the road to Sweet Home for twenty-two years as senior pastor. Do not be surprised if God ask you to give up your comfort zone or your secure and familiar surroundings to accomplish his will. Instead of God taking Abraham's son, He used the same boy to give Abraham a nation. You cannot be afraid to trust God with your most prized possessions. Material possessions should be our least concern. Jesus Christ let us know *"to seek ye first the kingdom of God and his righteousness and all these other things shall be added unto you"* (Matthew6:33). Our greatest reward will not be seen here in this life. It can only be seen in eternity. Because Abraham was willing to give all that he had to God, he was blessed with more than he could have imagined.

IN GENESIS 18 YOU WILL FIND THAT ISAAC was the promise child to come. The future factor played a role throughout Abraham's life. The Lord made a promise to Abraham he would have a son at 100 years old and Sarah at 90 years old. Abraham laughed in Genesis17, but the Lord appeared again in Genesis 18 and made the same promise. This time Sarai was named Sarah and she laughed. God asked the question "Is anything too hard for the Lord?" In Genesis chapter 21, the promise child (Isaac) is born. Abraham trusted God when he could not trace God. Jacob was Isaac's son and Abraham's grandson. Jacob's sons became the fathers of Israel's 12 tribes. Even when Jacob (also called "Israel") was dying in a strange land, he believed the

LOOKING FORWARD

promise that Abraham's descendants would be like the sand on the seashore and that Israel would become a great nation (Genesis 48:1-22). True faith helps us see beyond the grave.

JOSEPH, ONE OF JACOB'S SONS, WAS SOLD into slavery by his jealous brothers (Genesis 37). Eventually, Joseph was sold again, this time to an officer of the Pharaoh of Egypt. Because of his faithfulness to God, however, Joseph was given a top-ranking position in Egypt. Although Joseph could have used that position to build a personal empire, he remembered God's promise to Abraham. After he had been reconciled to his brothers, he brought his family to be near him, and requested that his bones be taken to the Promised Land when the Jews eventually left Egypt (Genesis 50:24 &25). Faith means trusting in God and doing what He wants, regardless of the circumstances. No matter what Joseph went through he kept his faith in the God of his future. We may not know what the future holds but we need to know the one that holds the future. "When I think of the future that God has in store for his church and his people, I can hardly contain myself. We must be willing to face the future with an attitude of gratitude and faith. God has promised to help us in time of need. The scripture lets us know that He will give us the strength and encouragement to face all of our tomorrows. We know that He has prepared wonderful things for those who trust Him! Remember this self-evaluation always led to sovereign elevation." We can see how bright the future can be when we can see beyond all the obstacles and lead forward. John Maxwell stated *"If you don't create the future you want, you must endure the future you have. Most people do not lead their life, they accept their life."* As a future visionary and leader, you cannot accept your life as normal, but must continue to work hard for a better future. The apostle Paul said, *"Brethren, I count not myself to have apprehended: but this one thing I do, forgetting those things which are behind, and reaching forth unto those things that are before, I press toward the mark for the prize of the high calling of God in Christ Jesus."* Future visionary thinkers know that they have to have a strategic plan to help them stay on course. He or she understand that strategic planning will make a difference. "Survey results show that 85 percent of churches which have grown off the plateau have reevaluated their programs and priorities during the past five years, as compared to 59 percent of churches which have remained on the plateau. Similar, 40 percent of breakout churches have developed a long-range plan, as compared to only 18 percent of continual plateau churches."

THE FIRST THING YOU MUST REMEMBER THAT this is a process. It is not an event, but an ongoing journey. "Strategic planning is an envisioning process. Rather than start with the present and work forward incrementally toward a mission and vision, you start with a clearly articulated, compelling mission and vision and work backwards to where you are. You envision the future and then ask how do, I get there? This is what makes it so different from conventional strategic planning or a long-range planning exercise. Long range planning is too incremental and does not work out anymore. You cannot edge forward, when things around you are changing quickly. You plan for five years out, and all has changed in six months, requiring a new plan. God uses a strategic envision process that does more than plan a hoped-for future; it helps you create the future now." God has said that he would supply all of our needs, according to His riches and glory in Christ Jesus. As visionary leaders we have to use God resources and look beyond the obstacles that life present. God's resources are his people, specifically their talents, time, and treasures. While God is not dependent on people, he has accomplished his purpose through people. First, he uses our talents. He has given each of us a unique design (Job 10:8-9: Psalm 119:73: Isaiah 29:16; 64:8). This design consists of spiritual gifts, talents, a passion, a temperament, and other factors (see Romans 12:3-8: 1Corinthians 12: Ephesians 4:1-16). God can use these characteristics for ministry. Second, God uses our time. None of us feels that he or she has enough time to accomplish all that should be done each day. We always seem to run out of time. However, God controls our time and provides us with the amount necessary to accomplish his program (Proverbs 16:3). Finally, God uses our treasure. All that we have comes from His gracious hand (2 Corinthians

9:10). And He gives us the privilege of investing our finances in building his kingdom and his church." Future focus leaders look for other resources besides what God has required. It is their relationship with God, that lines up their vision and their priorities.

When we get our spiritual insight in line with Gods vision for our lives we can see and do great things. That is when the snap shot of the future becomes clear. Powhatten James wrote, *"God must have insight into things spiritual. He must be able to see the mountain filled with the horses and chariots of fire; he must be able to interpret the written by the finger of God upon the walls of conscience; he must be able to translate the signs of the times into terms of their spiritual meaning; he must be able to draw aside, now and then, the curtain of things material and let mortals glimpse the spiritual glories which crown the mercy seat of God. The man of God must declare the pattern shown to him on the mount; he must utter the vision granted to him upon the isle of revelation...None of these can he do without spiritual insight."* When the future of the vision become clear, the energy rises in the leader and the organization. A clear and compelling vision along with a strategic envision play provides motivation as you journey along in life. It also create cause and foster risk taking. When the future vision is communicated well and others catch it, Leadership is legitimized sustained. "What has sustained Christians from the beginning of the church in the book of Acts up to today? One answer is a biblical, compelling vision. It encourages people to look beyond the mundane and the pain of ministry. It keeps a picture in front that distracts form what is and announces. It is the glue that holds the church together in turbulent times. All the trouble and grief we experience in this world while serving the Savior are trivial compared to the importance of what we are attempting for him. That picture, carried in our mental wallets, is one way God sustains us in the worst of times". As we look forward to the future the mental picture of the vision keeps us looking pass all the obstacles of life. God never promised us it would be easy, but he did tell us He will never leave us or forsake us. Even when things do not go the way we think, we can still trust

LOOKING FORWARD

God to bring our vision to pass. Staying committed to the process can become difficult with all the distraction and disruptions. However, if we commit our works unto the Lord, He will establish our thoughts. It is God who has to bring the future vision to pass. When we get self out of the way, we can watch God do great things in our life. When self is out of the way, you can look forward and see beyond the obstacles of life.

4
THE AUTHORITY FACTOR

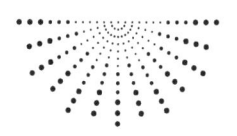

Authority is a major factor in the life of those that can look beyond the obstacles of life and continue to move forward. We all was born with an inherited gift from God. *"Having then gifts differing according to the grace given to us, whether prophecy, let us prophesy according to the proportion of our faith; or ministry, let us wait on ministering: he that give, let him do it with simplicity; he that rule, with diligence; he that show mercy, with cheerfulness"* (Romans 126-8). God's gift differ in nature and power according to His wisdom and goodness and not according to our faith. The measure of faith or the proportion of faith

LOOKING FORWARD

means that God will give the spiritual power necessary to carry out God given vision. We cannot, by our effort or will power, drum up the ability to be effective preacher, teachers, or servants.

LOOK AT THE LIST OF GIFTS THAT GOD HAS given to his people. Prophets are usually bold and articulate. Ministers (servers) are faithful and loyal. Teachers are clear thinkers. Preachers are exhorters that motivate others. Givers are generous and trusting. Administrators are good organizers and managers. Comforters are those that do not mind sharing their time to heal others. It would be impossible for one person to embody these gifts. A generous giver might fail as an administrator or an assertive prophet may not make a good counselor. *"Wherefore he said, when he ascended up on high, he led captivity captive, and gave gifts unto men"* (Ephesians 4:8). When we identify our own gifts, we can be an effective leader. Be grateful for the gifted people that God place around you instead of being envious or jealous. We are to let each other's strengths balance each other's weaknesses.

"Now there are diversities of gifts, but the same Spirit. And there are differences of administrations, but the same Lord. And there are diversities of operations, but the same God work. But the manifestation of the Spirit is given to every man to profit withal. For to one is given by the Spirit the word of wisdom; to another the word of knowledge by the same Spirit; to another faith by the same Spirit; to another the gift of healing by the same Spirit; to another the working of miracles; to another prophecy; to another discerning of spirits; to another diversity kinds of tongues; but all these work that one and selfsame Spirit, dividing to every man severally as he will" (1Corinthians 12:4-11). These spiritual gifts are given to each person by the Holy Spirit. The special ability that comes with each gift is to be used to minister to the needs of others. As we can see, there are many gifts and people have different gifts. Some people have more than one or two gifts. This does not make one gift superior to the other gift. Every good and perfect gift comes down from the Father above and is to be used for His glory. *"Now you are the body of Christ, and members. And God has set some in the church,*

LOOKING FORWARD

first apostles, secondarily prophets, thirdly teachers, after that miracles, then gifts of healing, helps, government, diversities of tongues. Are all apostles? Are all prophets? Are all teachers? Are all workers of miracles? Have all the gift of healing? Do all speak with tongues? Do all interpret? But covet the best gifts: And yet I show you a more excellent way" (1Corinthians 12:27-31). Paul is telling us that the best gifts are those that build up the body of Christ and help people look forward and see beyond the obstacles of life. It has already been stated that no gift is better than the other, but only what you do for Christ will last. He urges us to use our gifts to the glory of God. The gift that God has given each and every one of us is not for our own self-advancement. They were given to us to grow, develop, and advance others. We have these gifts and the power to use them. The problem occurs when we are not authorized to use these God given powers.

So, what we have to understand is the purpose of power and authority. These two words carry a lot of weight and carries similarities. However, these two words have different meaning, and there is a need for the future leader to know the difference. What good is it to have the gift or gifts, yet you do not have the power or authority to use them. Sure, we have the power, if we are a part of the family of God. *"To as many as believe on him to them he gave power to become the sons of God, even them that believe on his name"* (John 1:12). "What is this Holy Ghost power" and what does it mean to the future visionary leader. And if the believers have the power, then what is the problem? The problem is understanding authority and power and the difference between the two.

POWER IS DEFINED AS POSSESSION OF control or influence over others. It is the ability to act or produce an effect. After Jesus healed the paralyzed man in Matthew 9, he said in verse six *"That you may know that the Son of man has power on earth to forgive sins,"* (then said he to the sick of the palsy,) *"arise and take up thy bed and walk."* It's easy to tell someone his or her sins are forgiven; it's a lot more difficult to reverse a case of paralysis! Jesus backed up his words by healing the paralyzed man's legs. His action showed that his words were true; he had the power to forgive and to heal. Talk is cheap, but our words lack meaning is our actions do not back them up. We can say we love God or others, but if we are not taking practical steps to demonstrate that love, our words are empty and meaningless. How well do your actions back up what you say? In order for our words to back up our actions we not only need the power, but we need to be authorized to use the power. Another case of authority verse power took place when Jesus sent out the seventy disciples. In (Luke 1:19) Jesus said *"Behold I give you power to tread on serpents and scorpions, and over all the power of the enemy: and nothing shall by any means hurt you."* This again show how Jesus had power and he was authorized to empower others. When he spoke to the wind and sea, and said peace be still. The wind and the water ceased at his command. This again demonstrated Jesus' power and authority, even over nature. God has given us the power to become His son, but are we authorized to use that power. "Power is merely energy and ability, but authority is permission and right to use power. Power without authority is energy with authorization; it is illegal force. The key to success is not power alone but knowing and using authorized power. Someone acting with true authority empowers and protects people. True authority converts power into service." When there is no authorized leader, you end up with power struggles. The 95 percent theory is that 95 percent of all serious problems in the organization or church stem from some type of power struggle. "Almost every struggling church has at least one dysfunctional bully who goes out of the way to be a big fish in a small pond". Often, that is the primary reason the church is struggling. This person gets a sense of self-worth by keeping the church intimidated, either by action or money that little can happen without the person's approval. The sad thing is that most leaders know this person presents a stumbling block to the church's future, but they will not do anything about it. The church leaders ignore the bully thinking that is the Christian thing to do. In so doing they assist in the congregation's stunted growth or decline." This is a person that operates out of the boss spirit. This spirit is stub-

LOOKING FORWARD

born and rebellious to whatever the church or organization is trying to do. "The concept of the "boss spirit" is related to power, but its main attribute is the abuse of the position through manipulation. The word *manipulate* is defined as "to control or play upon by artful, unfair, or insidious means". The boss spirit is this, the ides that having authority means you can take advantage of people, order them around at will, and get them to do what you want through coercion. Such a perspective is unnatural and antithetical to true authority. When someone is in a leadership position embraces this false idea of authority, he engages in actions that intimidate, discriminate, exploit, oppress, suppress, and abuse people. Many people have either treated others according to the boss spirit or have experienced the receiving end, to a greater or less extent.

THE OPPOSITE OF THE BOSS SPIRIT IS TO USE authority for the good of all concerned and to seek others' cooperation and contributions rather than trying to maneuver them". When Jesus rose from the grave, He, Himself *de-*

clared "All power is given unto me in heaven and in earth. Go you therefore, and teach all nations, baptizing them in the name of the Father, Son, and the Holy Ghost: Teaching them to observe all things whatsoever I have commanded you: and lo, I am with you always, even unto the end of the world" (Matthew 28:18). God gave Jesus the authority over heaven and earth. It is on the basis of this authority, Jesus told his disciples to make other disciples, as they taught, preached, and baptized. With this same authority Jesus still commands us to go make disciples. Authority comes from the Latin word, auctor. Auctor simply means promoter, author, or originator. An author is the originator or a creator of something. And because God authorized His beloved son in whom He is well pleased to be the author and finisher of our faith. God is the ultimate authority. The word God means the supreme and ultimate reality. God is the perfect being in wisdom, goodness, and power. When an author create something, it has purpose, and the author desire is to communicate something. As a visionary leader, God created you with purpose. *"For I know the thoughts that I think toward you, said the Lord,*

LOOKING FORWARD

thoughts of peace, and not of evil, to give you an expected end" (Jeremiah 29:11). It is the authority of God that allows us to use His power to accomplish His will, and the vision or task that that He has given us. God supports His delegated authority by watching over His word to perform it. He becomes responsible for making sure that the authority He gave you succeeds. If you have real authority and delegate, it to someone, you will not leave the one you delegated the authority to for failure. *"The Lord will fulfill His purpose for me"* (Psalms 138:8). It is God who shared His authority with mankind from the beginning. God said, *"Let us make man in our image, in our likeness, and let them rule over the fish and the sea and the birds of the air, over the livestock, over all the earth, and over all the creatures that move along the ground. So, God created man in His own image, in the image of God he created him; male and female he created them"* (Genesis 1:26-27). God has given us the power of the Holy Spirit and his authority to accomplish great things for the kingdom. It is unfortunate that man from the beginning gave up his authority in the Garden of Eden and is still giving it away.

Adam and Eve did the opposite of what God told them to do because they chose power over the authority of God.

GOD HAS AN ENEMY, SATAN WHICH MEANS accuser or adversary. He is also called the devil and he tempted them to do this. Satan is a created angelic being who rebelled against God's authority himself. His goal is to cause humans to lose their true selves by forfeiting the precious life and authority that God has given to them. He tempted the first humans by asking them "Wouldn't you like to be like God?" Yet Adam and Eve were already like God; they were created in his image and reflected his nature. They had his delegated authority. But Satan wanted them to doubt who thy inherently were and to become something else, something unnatural. And this is how he has been tempting human beings ever since." All the things we see going on in this world is because man abandoned his authority. The God of this earth has caused man to turn their shared authority over to him. Satan lured one third of the angels to abandon their authority. *"And the angels which kept not their first es-*

tate (position of authority) but left their own habitation, he hath reserved in everlasting chains under darkness unto the judgment of the great" (Jude 1:6). Rebellion against God is what causes people to lose their shared authority. Jude gives us three examples of how we rebel against God. The children of God, although they were delivered from Egypt, refused to trust God and go into the promise land (Numbers 14:26-39). The angels that was once pure, holy, and singing in God's presence. Gave into pride and joined Satan to rebel against God (2Peter 2:2). The cities of Sodom and Gomorrah was destroyed because of wickedness and rebellion against God. We should learn from these examples that rebellion against God leads to destruction and loss of shared authority. If the chosen people of God, the angels He created, and entire cities could not escape, how shall we if we neglect so great of salvation and the God's shared authority. The cities that rebelled are destroyed, the angles kept in darkness, but the good news is that human beings do not have to remain in darkness. They can be restored to their natural place and restored to former shared authority. There should come a time in life you make a conscience decision to accept God's gift and grace to all that will accept it. To realize that we are fearful and wonderfully made, in his image and likeness, and belong to him.

THE AUTHORITY THAT GOD GIVES TO HIS children is to have a relationship where we do not just see the creator, but we now see Him as a Father. *"And because you are sons, God has sent forth the Spirit of His son into your hearts crying, Abba Father"* (Galatians 4:6). Jesus said, when you pray, say our Father which art in heaven. Hallowed be thy name. What a privilege it is to be called a son of God and to be authorized to use His power. *"He came unto his own, and his own received him not. But as many as received him, to them he gave power to become the sons of God, even to them that believe on his name"* (John 1:11-12). God has authorized the visionary leader to use His power through his son, Jesus Christ. *"Although he was a son, he learned obedience from what he suffered and, once made perfect, he became the source of eternal salvation for all who obey him"* (Hebrews 5:8-9). Christ was always morally perfect. By obeying, he demonstrated his perfection to us, not to God or to himself. In the Bible, perfection usually means completeness or maturity. By sharing our experience of suffering, Christ shared our human experience completely. He is now able to offer salvation to those who obey Him. See Philippians 2:5-11 for Christ attitude as he took on human form. The *"eternal salvation"* we have been offered means the elimination of a verdict on our sin. The setting aside of judgment, and the award of undeserved membership in God's family. It is a change in destiny, an awakening of hope, an overcoming of death. Salvation turns a person toward heaven and inaugurates a life of discipleship with the living Christ. It is God's vote for you, God's invitation to you. God's energy invested in you. Salvation is the reason you can smile in the morning and rest in the evening. God loves you, and you belong to him.

. . .

Someone might ask, "Why would God send His Son to be a sacrifice for us? Why would God experience punishment for us? Why would God raise Jesus from the dead and establish Him as King of Kings?" He did this to redeem us, because the authority we are carrying inside us is so awesome that He considered it worth His death. Do you understand that the earth needs you? It needs your purpose and your gift. It needs your authority." Jesus understood that the world needed his authority. For as the Father has life in himself, so he has granted the Son to have life in himself. And he has given him authority to judge because he is the Son of Man" (John 5:26-27). When you understand the authority that God has given you, your confidence will grow and your vision becomes clearer. *"Being confident in this very thing, that he that begun a good work in you will perform it until the day of Jesus Christ:"* (Philippians 1:6). We should be thanking God for his shared authority and take on responsibility to remain in it. "Everyone and everything must submit to someone or something in order to function and succeed. It is impossible to outgrow authority. We may transfer our accountability to different kinds of authority, such as, when a child grows up and moves out from under his parents' authority, starts his own family, and interacts with others in the world, but we never grow out of the need for authority itself. This is true for all of creation and in all human experience. Anyone who refuses to be governed by genuine authority is illegitimate and malfunctioning in the world." Jesus understood the need for authority itself, and he submitted to his own established law. In so doing he fulfilled the word he came not to destroy the law, but he fulfilled the law. Jesus submitted to being baptized to being because he knew that the secret to life is too constantly submit to God and his authority. Even when we do not understand His authority, we benefit from our submission. Our submission will lead us to a life we could have never imagined. But a lot of people never look forward to see beyond their obstacles. What they end up doing is submitting their shared authority to someone or something, rather than God. Because of the grace of God, they end up okay, however they missed the heavenly life that God wanted them to live on earth. Pastor Miller, A great man of God, always told me that if I can't see it in the spiritual, I will settle for what I see in the natural. When you settle for what you see in the natural, that's what you get: a natural life. But when you accept what you see in the super natural, you can live an abundant life. This abundant life is what Jesus promised and it comes with all the attributes of the Holy Spirit. Unfortunately, most people settle for the natural, and miss or did not accept what God was trying to show them in the spiritual. "Your success in your authority will you depend on your own ability to submit to genuine authority and to learn and serve". When a person does not know who they are in Christ, then they cannot submit to God's shared authority. Submission to authority will bring you spiritual power and protection.

IN MATTHEW 4:1 AFTER GOD AFFIRMED HIS beloved son, the bible states, *"Then was Jesus led by the Spirit into the desert to be tempted of the devil."* Had Jesus refused to be baptized by John before he went into the wilderness, Then Jesus would not have been able to with stand the temptation he faced. Jesus would have been acting in a way that does not line up with God's shared authority. Spiritual strength and the ability to with stand the enemy, comes from being obedient to God's ways and by remaining in His authority. When we remain in the authority of God, he gives us the faith and power to reach our goals. "The catalog of saints in Hebrews 11 is a study of vision and decision. They saw the vision, counted the cost, made their decision, and went into action. The same movement is evident in the lives of great missionary leaders. Carey saw the vision in Kettering and made his decision for India, though the difficulties of getting there loomed as high as heaven itself. Livingstone saw the vision in Dumbarton, made his decision, overcame all obstacles, and proceeded to Africa. Circumstances cannot frustrate such people, or difficulties deter him". As I said earlier, what made Jesus' ministry special was that he was under God's authority and had the power to fulfill his purpose. As God's son and ambassador, he only did what the Father did and said what he said. It is the spirit God that will help us to reach our desired goal. "Not only will you make life look easy by exercising your personal authority, but your life will also be easier because you will not be fighting against unnatural or unauthorized activities or environments". The leader that operates in the authority of God is able to look forward and see beyond the obstacles of life.

5
THE LEADERSHIP FACTOR

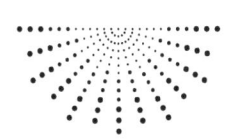

It has always been said that everything rises and falls on leadership. There and many definitions process whereby a person leads another person or a group of people to accomplish a common goal. As I said there are many definitions of leadership but the one, I like to use is, leadership is the God given ability to lead his people from where they are to where God wants them to be. God raised up Moses to go down to Egypt and lead His people from where they were to where He wanted them to be. When Moses gave God's message to the people, they were too discouraged to listen. The Hebrews didn't want to hear any more about God and his

Promises because the last time they listened to Moses all they got was more work and greater suffering. Sometimes a clear message from God is followed by a period when no change in the situation is apparent. During that time, seeming setbacks may turn people away from wanting to hear more about God. If you are a leader, don't give up. Keep bringing people God's message as Moses did. By focusing on God, who must be obeyed, rather than on the results to be achieved, good leaders see beyond temporary setbacks and reversals.

THINK HOW HARD IT MUST HAVE BEEN FOR Moses to bring God's message to Pharaoh when his own people had trouble believing it. He must have felt very alone. Moses obeyed God, however, and what a difference it made! When the chances for success appear slim, remember that anyone can obey God when the task is easy and everyone is behind it. Only those with persistent faith can obey when the task seems impossible. "Every visionary must go on a journey. Once you receive vision, you must learn to move the vision. Many people lose hope and faith in the

LOOKING FORWARD

journey process. It takes time, effort, favor, providence and grace to successfully make it through the journey of a visionary. Most importantly it requires stamina. But where does the visionary receive their encouragement? The presence of God serves as comforter and encourager to the vision while on this journey to victory. We find great help in the Word of God. We find encouragement in the word of God. We find comfort in the word of God. We find affirmation for our vision in the distance yet is so close to the ear of our hearts. A voice that offers us the words we need to continue our journey. "The same voice that Moses heard when in the burning bush is the same one Moses heard when the journey got hard. The fire in bush that burn and was not consumed is now burning in the heart of Moses. It give him the strength to get God's people from where they are to where God wants them to be. They journey was hard but God used this leader to do extraordinary things. Six hundreds Egyptian war chariots were bearing down on the helpless Israelites, who were trapped between the mountains and the sea. The war chariots each carried two people----one to drive and one to fight. They were made of wood or leather cab placed over two wheels and pulled by horses. These were the armored tanks of Bible times. But even their power was no match for God, who destroyed both the chariots and their soldiers. Trapped against the sea, the Israelites faced the Egyptian army sweeping in for the kill. The Israelites thought they were doomed. After watching God's powerful hand deliver them from the Egypt, their only response was fear, whining, and despair. Where was their trust in God? Israel had to learn from repeated experience that God was able to help them. God has preserved these examples in the Bible so that we can learn to trust Him the first time. By focusing on God's faithfulness in the past we can faced crises with confidence rather than fear and complaining. This is the first instance of grumbling and complaining by the Israelites. Grumbling would become a major problem for the people on this journey. Their lack of faith in God is starting. Yet how often do we find ourselves doing the same thing--- complaining over inconveniences or discomforts? The Israelites were about to learn some tough lessons. Had they trusted God, they would have been

LOOKING FORWARD

spared much grief. The people were hostile and despairing, but Moses encouraged then to watch the wonderful way God would rescue them. Moses had a positive attitude! When it looked as if they were trapped, he called God to intervene. We may not be chased by an army, but we may still feel trapped. Instead of giving into despair, we should adopt Moses' attitude to *"stand still, and see the salvation of the Lord."* The Lord told Moses to stop praying and get moving! Prayer must have a vital place in our lives, but there is also a place for action. Sometimes we know what to do, but we pray for more guidance as an excuse to postpone doing it. If we know what we should do, then it is time to get moving. So, Moses got to moving and led the children of Israel to the promise land.

When the children of Israel got there, they lost their faith again. By this time Moses is up in age. However, Moses being a future visionary leader had prepared Joshua to take the reign. All leaders should see their work continue on in the future through the next person that God has pointed out for them to prepare. Joshua succeeded as Israel's leader. *What qualifications did he have to become the leadership of the nation?* (1) *God appointed him.* (Numbers 27:18-23). (2) *He was one of the only two living eyewitnesses to the Egyptian plagues and the Exodus from Egypt.* (3) *He was Moses personal assistant for 40 years.* (4) *Of the 12 spies, only he and Caleb showed complete confidence that God would help them conquer the land.*

BECAUSE JOSHUA HAD ASSISTED MOSES FOR many years, he was well prepared to take over the leadership of the nation. Changes in leadership are common in many organizations. At such times, a smooth transition is essential for the establishment of the new administration. This doesn't happen unless new leaders are trained. If you are currently in a leadership position, begin preparing someone to take your place. Then, when you leave or are promoted, operations can continue to run efficiently. If you desire to be a leader, learn from others so you will be prepared when the opportunity comes.

. . .

LOOKING FORWARD

JOSHUA'S NEW JOB CONSISTED OF LEADING more than two million people into a strange new land and conquering it. What a challenge---even for a man of Joshua's caliber! Ever new job is a challenge. Without God it can be frightening. With God it can be a great adventure. Just as God was with Joshua, he is with us as we face our new challenges. We may not conquer nations, but every day we face tough situations, difficult people, and temptations. God promises, however, that he will never abandon us or fail to help us, regardless of how we feel or fail. By asking God to direct us we can conquer many of life's problems that we face. The Lord directed the steps of Joshua. *"Now after the death of Moses the servant of the Lord it came to pass, that the Lord spoke unto Joshua the son of Nun, Moses's minister, saying, Moses my servant is dead; now therefore arise, go over this Jordan, thou and all this people, unto the land which I do give them, even to the children of Israel. Every place that the sole of your foot shall tread upon, that have I given unto you, as I said unto Moses"* (Joshua 1:1-3). After the children of Israel had wandered in the wilderness for forty years, a new generation is ready to march into the promise land. But God had to prepare Joshua and the nation of Israel, by teaching them the importance of courage and faith. *"Be strong and of good courage: for unto this people shalt thou divide for an inheritance the land, which I swore unto their fathers to give them. Only be thou strong and very courageous, that thou may observe to do according to all the law, which Moses my servant commanded thee: turn not from it to the right hand or to the left, that thou may prosper whithersoever thou go. This book of the law shall not depart out of thy mouth; but thou shalt meditate therein day and night, that thou mightiest observe to do according to all that is written therein: for then thou shalt make thy way prosperous, and then thou shalt have good success. Have not I commanded thee? Be strong and of good courage; be not afraid, neither be thou dismayed: for the Lord thy God is with thee whithersoever thou got"* (Joshua 1:6-9). Many people thank prosperity and success come from having power, influential personal contacts, and a desire to get ahead. But the strategy for gaining prosperity that God taught Joshua goes against such criteria. He

LOOKING FORWARD

told Joshua that to succeed he must (1). *Be strong and brave because the task ahead would not be easy.* (2) *Obey God's Law.* (3) *Constantly read and study God's Word.* To be successful, follow God's words to Joshua. You may not succeed by the world standards, but you will be a success in God eyes and his opinion is most important. Not only do we find success with God, we also become significant in God eyes.

JOSHUA WAS SUCCESSFUL IN LEADING THE children of Israel into the promise land. Joshua success and significance came from following the Lord. He understood that to be a good leader, you had to be a good follower. He watched and learned as he saw Moses follow God. Joshua followed God across the Jordon River, to Jericho, Ai and on into the promise land. Through it all Joshua made up his mind to wholly follow the Lord. *"Now therefore fear the LORD, and serve him in sincerity and in truth: and put away the gods which your fathers served on the other side of the flood, and in Egypt, and serve ye the Lord. And if it seem evil unto you to serve the*

LORD, choose you this day whom ye will serve; whether the gods which your fathers served that where on the other side of the flood, or the gods of the Amorites, in whose land ye dwell: but as for me and my house, we will serve the LORD." (Joshua 24: 14&15). Joshua reminded the people of God's goodness and his provision to them by reviewing past times when God had blessed then. Reviewing past blessings can encourage us to continue to serve faithfully. When you need a reminder of God's love, review how God has blessed you in the past. Then turn to the Bible and see how unchanging his love is. The people had to decide whether they would obey the Lord, who had proven his trustworthiness or obey the local gods which were idols. It's easy to follow false gods and to slip into silent rebellion when going about life your own way. In taking a defiant stand for the Lord, Joshua showed Spiritual leadership. God chose Joshua, and prepared him for the journey as Israel's visionary leader, after Moses died.

. . .

LOOKING FORWARD

GOD IS STILL SEARCHING FOR SPIRITUAL leaders that hear his voice and follow him. *"The Lord sought out a man after his own heart and appointed him leader of his people"* (Samuel 13:14). "The Bible shows us that when God does find a person who is ready to lead, to commit to full discipleship and take on responsibility for others, that person is used to the limit. Such leaders still have shortcomings and flaws, but despite them, they become spiritual leaders. Such was Moses, Gideon, and David". All of these men accomplished great things for the kingdom of God, despite their flaws. If we are to be visionary leaders, we have to be spiritual. To keep the faith and stay focused on the future we must have more than mere human strength. As the visionary leader surrenders to the Holy Spirit, He (Holy Spirit) takes control and then flow through the spiritual leader to others. "Spiritual leadership requires superior spiritual power, which can never be generated by self. There is no such thing as a self-made spiritual leader. A true leader influences others spiritually only because the Spirit works in and through him to a greater degree than in those he leads." We talked about the gifts of the Spirit earlier, and how everyone have gifts. The Spiritual visionary leader has the responsibility to help others discover their gift and develop them. This requires that the visionary leader has the fruit of the spirit that Paul talked about in the book of Galatians. In order to move God's people from where they are to where God wants them to be requires super natural power. He or she has to deal with Satan attacks, family matters, job problems, church issues, and so on, and still stay focused on the vision ahead. To be filled with the Spirit is to be controlled by the Spirit. The Christian leader's mind, emotions, and physical strength all become available for the Spirit to guide and use. Under the Spirit's control, natural gifts of leadership are lifted to their highest power, sanctified for holy purpose. Through the work of the now ungrieved and unhindered Spirit, all the fruit of the Spirit start to grow in the leader's life. His witness is more winsome, service is steadier, and testimony more powerful. All real Christian service is but the expression of the Spirit's power through believers yielded to him" (John 7:37-39). God takes whatever gift that He gives each visionary leader and blends it with the Holy Spirit to accomplish supernatural things for his kingdom and his glory. This type of spiritual visionary leader is totally dependent upon the Holy Spirit and totally accountable to God. He or she can influence people in any arena, they are not confined just to the church. The spiritual visionary leader works from God's perspective and on God's agenda. "There is no such thing as a self-made spiritual leader. Spiritual ends requires Spiritual means, and spiritual means come only by the Holy Spirit." *It is God who put the visionary in a position of leadership and it is God who keeps them there to complete His will.* Jesus always reminded the disciples that he came not to do his will, but the will of the Father. People can have all the talents, take as much leadership training as they want to, but they will not become spiritual leaders unless God place them and equip them for the task. "The fact that God can bring character development and personal growth out of any situation is conditional on people's willingness to submit to God's will. God is sovereign over every life, but those who yield their will to Him will be shaped according to his purposes. *When God directs a life for his purposes, all of life is a school. No experience, good or bad is ever wasted* (Rom. 8:28). *God doesn't squander people's time. He doesn't ignore their pain. He brings not only healing but growth out of even the worst experiences.* Every relationship can be God's instrument to mature a person's character. The world can offer the best theories on leadership and provide the most extensive training possible, but unless God set the agenda for a leader's life, that person, though thoroughly educated, will not be an effective spiritual leader." He or she understands that their success can only come from following the Holy Spirit. The Holy Spirit leads and guides us in ways that only God know. Our service as spiritual visionary leaders is to follow Him and be obedient to what He says.

SPIRITUAL VISIONARY LEADERS UNDERSTAND the importance of prayer. They understand that the vision must be bathed in prayer. Prayer is the key to success and faith unlock the door for opportunities. Even when the journey gets tough, we as spiritual visionary leaders should pray and not faint. They also understand that it is no easy task before them. Trying to understand what God is saying and doing, while trying to communicate it to the followers as clear as possible a glimpse of the future. Spiritual visionaries understand that they are called to serve and not to be served. In the midst of all that the spiritual visionary leader face, they still maintain a positive attitude. *"Spiritual leaders understand the importance of a positive attitude as an effective leadership tool, but they remain optimistic not because doing so is a vital practice but because they are in touch with God. This is why spiritual leaders need to spend as much time in in the conscience presence of God. Only after clearly understanding who God is, can leaders gain a proper perspective on their situation. A glimpse into the scriptures provides ample support for a positive attitude."* The spiritual visionary leader know that their attitude determines their latitude. A positive attitude keeps you looking forward and seeing beyond the obstacles of life.

AFTERWORD

The purpose of the visionary leader is to look at things through the lens of the Lord Jesus Christ and see the blessing of God. This is for those who God has saved and commissioned them to go teach other faithful people that will teach others. *"And the things that thou have heard of me among many witnesses, the same commit thou to faithful men, who shall be able to teach others also"* (1 Timothy 2:2). The visionary leader follows the examples of the Lord and savior Jesus Christ. They are called a follow-first leader. The Bible is clear that Jesus came to follow, call followers, and follow the will of the Father in his second

AFTERWORD

coming (Mark 13:32). The thread of following the Lord is woven through out the Old and New Testament Scriptures. As following the will of the Father was the purpose and teaching of the Lord Jesus Christ, so ministers and leaders within the church need to begin with a follow first perspective as we follow the head of the church (Ephesians 5:23). The follow-first leader embraces the vision that God has given him and challenges the followers to rally to the leaders' vision and assume responsibility, and seek to make the leaders vision come to pass. When this happens all glory go to God who is the supreme leader.

The leader that is looking forward and seeing beyond the obstacles of life, stay focused on the vision. The follow first perspective keep the leader focused because he or she is willing to love and follow God. They also commit to other followers that follows the Lord Jesus Christ. The Lord Jesus commanded the followers to make other follow first leaders. *"And Jesus came and spoke unto them saying, all power is given unto me in heaven and in earth. Go you therefore, and teach all nations,*

AFTERWORD

baptizing them in the name of the Father, and of the Son, and of the Holy Spirit. Teaching them to observe all things whatsoever I have commanded you, and lo, I am with you always, even unto the end of the world" (Matthew 28:18-20). The focused visionary leader follows the Lord Jesus Christ with a strong commitment to seeing his will done. "Originally, we were all 'wired' to honor God and find fulfillment by following the will of the Creator. Sin entered the world because our first parents refused to follow God's commands, and since that time, the focus of human fulfillment has been myopically placed on one's own personal fulfillment. Rather than reveling in being a follower of the commands of God our sinful natures revel in following the desires of the flesh. But please note, we are always following, because human beings were created to follow." Our success depends on who we decide to follow. As future visionary leaders, we should follow the one who knows and holds the future in his hand. Jesus is not only the greatest leader to ever live, he also is the greatest follower to ever live. We will never reach our full potential or accomplish our goal, without the help

AFTERWORD

of the Holy Spirit. *"I can of myself do nothing. As I hear, I judge; and my judgment is righteous, because I do not see my own will but the will of the Father who sent me"* (John 5:30). As said before, it is the power of God working in ordinary people to accomplish great things. When we allow the Holy Spirit to lead, the future is much brighter and we see clearer.

When we look forward and see beyond the obstacles of life, we are looking into our future. Jesus always looked forward to the future, when He would be reunited with his Father. As He tried to prepare the disciples for His departure here on earth, He spoke of the future. *"Let not your heart be troubled: you believe in God believe also in me. In my Father's house are many mansions: If it were not so, I would have told you. I go to prepare a place for you, and I will come again, and receive you unto myself; that where I am there you may be also"* (John14:1-3). Jesus not only spoke of the future; He also spoke of eternal life. Jesus shows us that the way to eternal is certain. All we have to do is believe in Him and look forward to a brighter future.

AFTERWORD

Jesus knew it would not be an easy journey, however He stayed focused on the Father's will and the future. We should look to the future as Jesus did, seeing beyond all we go through, to the expected end that God has for us. By fighting through the difficult times and overcoming the obstacles of life. This gives us the opportunity to learn from experience and grow in grace.

When a child of God understands the authority that God has given them, they can lead others forward without the fear of failure. This shared authority will help to build fellowship and follow-ship. Without fellowship and follow-ship, the leader is just taking a stroll in life. Leaders need to have followers and followers need to have a leader. "Authority is designed to protect its product, not to restrict them. The Creator's authority establishes the boundaries, limitations, and references that protect us from misuse, abuse, and self-destruction. When our first human parents abandon their authority, they self-destructed, and we still experience the effects of that decision today. Jesus himself couldn't be without a covering of authority from God the

AFTERWORD

Father. We must continually remind ourselves that we need to be covered by authority so that we can also protect others and keep them safe". The spiritual visionary leader must recognize what true authority is and who it comes from. That is the only way that their natural gifts will blend with their spiritual gifts to accomplish the desired outcome. When these gifts are blended together you no longer feel intimidated by others. That is when you become the servant leader that God wants you to be. You can then live out your life with purpose and watch others transform into who God wants them to be. God wants us to do great things for his kingdom and be the greatest leader-follower we can be.

Great leaders are not necessarily the one who do the greatest things, but are the ordinary ones that do extraordinary things. Those who have great leadership skills are strong in the Lord but not rude: kind but not weak: bold but not bullish: thoughtful but not lazy: humble but not timid: proud but not arrogant: have a sense of humor but do not like folly. They seize every opportunity to change things for the better, gratifying some people and astonishing others. These are the leaders that lead forward and overcome the obstacles of life. They lead forward because they are looking forward to seeing beyond the obstacles of life.

THANK YOU

Thank you for purchasing and reading this book, Looking Forward: Seeing Beyond The Obstacles. I pray that every part of your life is filled with God's love, joy, peace, kindness and overflowing blessings.

I leave you with this special message from our Heavenly Father.

The words you are about to experience are true, for they come from the very heart of God. He loves YOU. And He is the Father you have been looking for all your life. This is His love letter to you.

My Beloved Child...

THANK YOU

You may not know me, but I know everything about you.
Psalm 139:1
I know when you sit down and when you rise up.
Psalm 139:2
I am familiar with all your ways.
Psalm 139:3
Even the very hairs on your head are numbered.
Matthew 10:29-31
For you were made in my image.
Genesis 1:27
In me you live and move and have your being.
Acts 17:28
For you are my offspring.
Acts 17:28
I knew you even before you were conceived.
Jeremiah 1:4-5
I chose you when I planned creation.
Ephesians 1:11-12
You were not a mistake,
for all your days are written in my book.
Psalm 139:15-16
I determined the exact time of your birth and where you would live.

Acts 17:26
You are fearfully and wonderfully made.
Psalm 139:14
I knit you together in your mother's womb.
Psalm 139:13
And brought you forth on the day you were born.
Psalm 71:6
I have been misrepresented by those who don't know me.
John 8:41-44
I am not distant and angry,
but am the complete expression of love.
1 John 4:16
And it is my desire to lavish my love on you.
1 John 3:1
Simply because you are my child and I am your Father.
1 John 3:1
I offer you more than your earthly father ever could.
Matthew 7:11
For I am the perfect father.
Matthew 5:48
Every good gift that you receive comes from my hand.
James 1:17

THANK YOU

For I am your provider and I meet all your needs.
Matthew 6:31-33
My plan for your future has always been filled with hope.
Jeremiah 29:11
Because I love you with an everlasting love.
Jeremiah 31:3
My thoughts toward you are countless as the sand on the seashore.
Psalm 139:17-18
And I rejoice over you with singing.
Zephaniah 3:17
I will never stop doing good to you.
Jeremiah 32:40
For you are my treasured possession.
Exodus 19:5
I desire to establish you with all my heart and all my soul.
Jeremiah 32:41
And I want to show you great and marvelous things.
Jeremiah 33:3
If you seek me with all your heart, you will find me.
Deuteronomy 4:29

Delight in me and I will give you the desires
of your heart.
Psalm 37:4
For it is I who gave you those desires.
Philippians 2:13
I am able to do more for you than you could
possibly imagine.
Ephesians 3:20
For I am your greatest encourager.
2 Thessalonians 2:16-17
I am also the Father who comforts you in all
your troubles.
2 Corinthians 1:3-4
When you are brokenhearted, I am close
to you.
Psalm 34:18
As a shepherd carries a lamb,
I have carried you close to my heart.
Isaiah 40:11
One day I will wipe away every tear from
your eyes.
Revelation 21:3-4
And I'll take away all the pain you have
suffered on this earth.
Revelation 21:3-4
I am your Father, and I love you even as I
love my son, Jesus.

THANK YOU

John 17:23
For in Jesus, my love for you is revealed.
John 17:26
He is the exact representation of my being.
Hebrews 1:3
He came to demonstrate that I am for you, not against you.
Romans 8:31
And to tell you that I am not counting your sins.
2 Corinthians 5:18-19
Jesus died so that you and I could be reconciled.
2 Corinthians 5:18-19
His death was the ultimate expression of my love for you.
1 John 4:10
I gave up everything I loved that I might gain your love.
Romans 8:31-32
If you receive the gift of my son Jesus, you receive me.
1 John 2:23
And nothing will ever separate you from my love again.
Romans 8:38-39
Come home and I'll throw

the biggest party heaven has ever seen.
Luke 15:7
I have always been Father, and will always be Father.
Ephesians 3:14-15
My question is…Will you be my child?
John 1:12-13
I am waiting for you.
Luke 15:11-32

Love, Your Dad.
Almighty God

ABOUT THE AUTHOR

Dr. Jeffery R. Wimbush, Sr. serves as the Senior Pastor of the Sweet Home Missionary Baptist Church in Hiram, GA. He completed his Diploma in Biblical Studies at Carver Bible College, and a Diploma in Criminal Justice Technology at Southern Crescent Technical College. He received his Bachelor of Art in Leadership and Administration from Beulah Heights University, Master of Art in Leadership from Luther Rice College & Seminary and Doctorate of Organizational Leadership from Restoration Theological Seminary. He joined the John Maxwell Leadership Team in 2019 and received his Leadership certification from Samuel Chand Leadership Institute in 2020.

Honors and Awards
Governor's Award (State of Georgia) 2017
Avr'i Entertainment Lifetime Achievement Award 2015
Gospel Choice Award 100 Most Influential Pastors in Georgia 2014
Avr'i Entertainment Lifetime Achievement Award 2013
Honorary Doctorate St. James Christian College 2011
Gospel Choice Award Top 10 Most Influential Pastors in Atlanta 2011
Mt. Moriah Excellence Award in Leadership 2011
Dr. Samuel Chand Servant Leader Award 2008

You may connect with Dr. Jeffery R. Wimbush, Sr.
at the following:
Website: www.godsgoodgroup.com

- facebook.com/jeffery.wimbush
- instagram.com/wimbushjefferydr
- linkedin.com/in/dr-jeffery-wimbush-8aa15032

ALSO BY DR. JEFFERY R. WIMBUSH, SR.

Leading Forward: Overcoming The Obstacles Of Life

You may purchase at Amazon.com

or contact

Dr. Jeffery R. Wimbush, Sr. at www.godsgoodgroup.com

NOTES

Blackaby, Henry & Richard. (2001). *Spiritual Leadership: Moving People on to God's Agenda.* Nashville, TN. B&H Publishing Group.

Chad, Sam. (2017). *First Focus: Finding Clarity in a Chaotic World.* Atlanta, Ga. Sam Chand.

Chad, Sam. (2017). *Future Faith: Shaping today's Ministry for Tomorrow's Opportunities.* Atlanta, GA. Sam Chand.

Flippin, William E. (2018). *20/20 Vision for the Victor: Motivational Words for the Victim.* Columbia, SC. Made in the USA.

NOTES

Frazee, Randy. (2011). *The Heart of the Story: God's Masterful Design to Restore His People.* Grand Rapids, MI. Zondervan.

Malphurs, Aubrey. (2013). *Advanced Strategic Planning: A 21st-Centrury Model for Church and Ministry Leaders.* Grand Rapids, MI. Baker Books.

Malphurs, Aubrey. (2003). *Being Leaders: The Nature of Authentic Christian Leadership.* Grand Rapids, MI. Baker Books.

Munroe, Dr. Myles. (2018). *Becoming a Leader: How to Develop and Release your Unique Gifts.* New Kensingtons, PA. Whitaker House.

Munroe, Dr. Myles. (2011). *The Purpose and Power of Authority: Discovering the Power of Your Personal Domain.* New Kensingtons, PA. Whitaker House

Munroe, Dr. Myles. (2003). *The Principles and Power of Vision: Keys to Achieving Personal and Corporate Destiny.* New Kensingtons, PA. Whitaker House.

Northouse, Peter. (2010). *Leadership: Theory and Practice Fifth Edition.* Thousand Oaks, CA. Sage Publications.

Ricketson, Rusty. (2014). *Follower First: Rethinking Leading in the Church.* Cumming, GA. Heartworks Publications.

Sanders, J. Oswald. (1994). *Spiritual Leadership: Principles of Excellence for Every Believer.* Chicago, IL. Moody Press.

Wood, Gene. (2001). *Leading Turnaround Churches.* St. Charles, IL. Church Smart Resources.

Made in the USA
Columbia, SC
23 April 2025